Table of Contents

Rottweiler Puppy Training 1

Bringing Home a New Rottweiler Puppy 3

Characteristics of Your Rottweiler Puppy 5

New Rottweiler Puppy Supplies You Must Have 7

Best Ways to Puppy Proof Your Home or Apartment 10

How to Potty Train a New Rottweiler Puppy 13

The ABC's of How to Feed a Rottweiler Puppy Properly 15

How Much Should I Feed My New Rottweiler Puppy 18

Puppy Training - 7 Most Important Words Your Rottweiler Puppy Should Know 19

How to Brush Your Puppy's Teeth So They Will Look Forward to it Every Time 22

Here is the Right Way to Start Bathing Your New Rottweiler Puppy 26

Puppy Air Travel -The Most Current Guidelines You May Not Know 29

Top 4 Reasons Why You Need Pet Insurance 31

10 Games You Can Play With Your Rottweiler Puppy 34

How to Teach Your Rottweiler Puppy Tricks 39

A Puppy's 10 Commandments 41

Bringing Home a New Rottweiler Puppy

Bringing home a new Rottweiler puppy can be a fun and memorable time. It can also be a lot of work filled with a whole new set of responsibilities. This guide will help you maneuver through those first few weeks and months with your new best friend.

You will learn everything you need to know so that you are well prepared from what supplies you will need and how to puppy proof your home so your Rottweiler is safe, to potty training, what food to feed and how much, bathing tips, pros and cons of puppy insurance and more.

Before you are finished you will learn the best ways to teach your new Rottweiler puppy tricks and know 10 really fun games you and your Rottweiler puppy can play together.

Finally, we will finish with a very poignant Puppies Ten Commandments.

You will find this a very helpful and thorough guide, essential to making sure the transition for you and your family and new Rottweiler puppy is as positive and successful as possible.

Characteristics of Your Rottweiler Puppy

Rottweiler's are large, powerful and muscular dogs. There are many words people use to describe this breed of dog chief among them include: confident, calm, courageous, self assured, not shy, highly intelligent and sensible.

With their family they are loving and affectionate. With strangers they don't make friends immediately and are more indiscriminant. They tend to take a more wait and see attitude, sizing up a new person first.

Despite all the great qualities of the Rottweiler this is a pet that requires a lot of work. Especially in the puppy stages, the first couple of years, it is important to train and socialize this dog properly so it learns manners and its natural aggressive nature is tamed.

There is also a fairly negative perception with this dog and the unknowing public. Many people are fearful of Rottweiler's. Also, it can be hard to get insurance for your home with his type of dog. Even some cities have a ban against Rottweiler's.

Despite these challenges, the Rottweiler can be a great pet.

As a puppy they are quite lively and active. That usually continues for the first three years. As they grow older they mature into a more calm, devoted and loving pet.

What determines the temperament of a Rottweiler are three factors: breeding, obedience training and amount of socialization given at a young age.

It is essential to start obedience training and socialization of your "Rotty" as a puppy. The earlier you do this, the better it will be for you and your dog. The time you spend training your Rottweiler will be time well spent. You will develop a bond and can show your dog that the leader of the pack is you. Most Rottweilers are inclined toward dominance and will test for position in the family pecking order, but they will respect an assertive owner who knows how to lead a strong-minded dog.

It will be important to keep your training sessions short and always be positive. Positive reinforcement works very well with this breed. These are sensitive animals and harsh will not work well.

Training should be challenging also—these are intelligent dogs. They need mental stimulation as well as physical challenges on a daily basis. Rottweilers will enjoy playing dog games with their master.

You will find some fun games Rottweiler's enjoy playing later in this book. If you want more Dog Games, there is another Kindle book that makes a perfect companion to this one. It has lots of Dog Gamesin it that are perfect for you and your Rottweiler. You can learn more about it by clicking here.

Young Rottweilers need enough exercise to keep them lean, but not so much that their growing bones, joints, and ligaments are over-stressed and damaged. Adult Rottweilers need enough exercise to keep them in shape, but not miles of running, and never in hot or humid weather -- their black coat makes them prone to overheating.

Since you need to minimize their exercise, young Rottweilers can be rambunctious. They will romp with uncoordinated gawkiness all over your house. You need to substitute extra quantities of companionship and supervision at this time. Otherwise, left alone, young Rottweilers become bored and destructive -- and their powerful jaws can destroy your living room.

A few things to consider about Rottweliers is that they can be gassy and snore. They also have the tendency to slobber after eating and drinking. Even though they are a short haired dog, they actually shed quite a bit.

They can be aggressive with other dogs of the same sex, and while many Rottweilers live peacefully with the family cat, other individuals are predatory toward cats.

Their biggest health concerns as they grow older include: Health Concerns: Hip and Elbow Dysplasia, Aortic Stenosis, Cataracts, Diabetes Mellitus, and certain types of cancer.

New Rottweiler Puppy Supplies You Must Have

If you are bringing home a new rottweiler puppy there are certain puppy supplies you must bring home with you. A new rottweiler puppy is cute and the decision to bring one home is often emotional, but you can't forget there are certain things you must have.

The move away from its mother and litter mates can be difficult at first for the new puppy. If you want that transition to be as smooth as possible here are the correct puppy supplies you must have. Use this as a new puppy checklist.

It is best to obtain these puppy supplies before bringing your new best friend home. Once the new puppy is home things can get very hectic.

First make sure you have two bowls. One bowl will be for water and the other will be for the puppy's food. The best type of bowl is stainless steel. These will not chip or crack like glass, ceramic or even plastic. This is really a completely separate topic, but be sure to feed your new puppy the same food it has been eating for the first few days and slowly add a well selected dry kibble type puppy food over the next couple of weeks.

A pet gate is also a must have puppy supply item. Be sure to designate an area where the puppy can safely roam free and close off this area with a puppy gate, also called an indoor dog gate. Make sure this area has nothing the new puppy can chew on that will be hazardous.

Every puppy needs something to chew on that belongs to them. It is in their nature to chew-so make sure you give your new dog a chew toy that will satisfy their needs. If you do not give them something that they know is okay to chew they will find something else and that won't make you very happy.

Your new pet will need a bed. Often for the first few weeks a box with blankets or towels will work very well. The puppy will prefer to sleep in an area where it feels secure, so don't make the bed area too big. As the dog grows then it will be time to invest in a nice bed, but let it get through the chewing stage first.

A hot water bottle and a ticking clock can often be a pretty decent substitute for the pup's mother. Put this in the bed area and that should help with the new transition at least for the first few days.

A collar and leash for your new dog is a good idea. Just make sure the collar is adjustable so it doesn't grow out of it too fast. The earlier in its life you can introduce a collar and leash is a very good idea.

Something else you should also consider is pet insurance. Your new dog will have accidents and become ill just like a human. Pet insurance makes going to the vet very inexpensive and in the long run your pet will receive better care throughout its life.

Best Ways to Puppy Proof Your Home or Apartment

Keeping your new rottweiler puppy safe is very important. Bringing a new puppy home to roam around is just like having a little infant child that just learned to walk. They like to explore and get into everything. As a result you must do things to make your house puppy safe. Here's what to do to make your house safe for a new puppy.

You should puppy proof your home well before you bring your new pet home. By having your home prepared for the new arrival you will insure its safety and prevent emergencies that could be life threatening.

First you need to decide where in your house the puppy will be allowed walk about. It is a good idea to put up barriers so certain areas are off limits and there is no worry of your new best friend going where it shouldn't.

Now that you have a designated area for the puppy you need to inspect it carefully for anything that may cause problems.

The best way to do this is to look at your house from the puppy's perspective. Crawl around and look at everything that might seem enticing to the new pup or pose a hazard.

Puppies are naturally very curious and will get into just about anything that is on the floor or within their height. Electrical cords or telephone cables need to be removed or taped higher than the new puppy's reach. If a puppy chews into an electrical cord it can be lethal or they can get very serious burns. They can easily get tangled in phone cords and possibly strangle also.

Take caution to remove any objects that might be on low areas like coffee tables. Small decorative pieces, books, magazines-- anything of this nature should be removed from the table as it might look good to chew or could fall of.

As you crawl around looking for objects look for anything that might be small enough that could be chewed or even swallowed that could pose a hazard just as if it would for a small child.

Rottweiler puppies love to chew. It is in their nature so there isn't much you can do to stop that. Be sure to remove anything they could get to that they should not be chewing. You should leave them appropriate chew toys designed for puppies, however.

Keep in mind that puppies love to swallow what they chew. Why just the other day, watching television there was a story about a family that kept losing their baby pacifiers. They had a feeling their new puppy might be chewing them-but they didn't think it was possible that it could be swallowing them. The dog was taken to the vet and x-rays showed it had 15 pacifiers in its stomach! Now of course, if you are like me you may be wondering, new baby....new puppy... hmmmm... what was that family thinking? But that's a whole different story.

There are many house plants that are not good for puppies. As a good rule of thumb, remove all house plants from the areas where the new puppy will roam.

You should also be careful that all household cleaners be stored outside of the puppy's reach. Many items like: insecticides, mothballs, antifreeze, fertilizers, insect poisons, and rat poisons can be fatally dangerous to dogs.

If the new puppy will be allowed to roam in the bathroom, be sure to keep the toilet lid down. Many cleaners used to keep the toilet bowl sanitized can be dangerous.

In summary, the best way to puppy proof your home is to do it crawling around from their perspective. Look for low hanging objects and keep in mind: anything that could be harmful to a small child could also be bad for your new rottweiler puppy.

How to Potty Train a New Rottweiler Puppy

It does not need to be difficult to potty train a new rottweiler puppy. You just have to have patience and understanding and a designated area where you want them to learn it is okay to go to the bathroom.

It is important to remember that going to the bathroom is natural for a puppy. It will have to do it several times a day and will make mistakes at first.

You should begin potty training the very first day you bring your new puppy home. Keep in mind that they will need to go every time the urge hits them and that is going to happen a lot. So it will be necessary for someone to watch your new best friend as much as possible, at least in the first few days.

Generally speaking a rottweiler puppy will need to go to the bathroom immediately after it takes from a nap, immediately after eating or drinking and after playtime. On these occasions pick your puppy up and take them to the area you want them to use to go potty. If they roam outside of the area just pick them up and bring them back.

When they do go to the bathroom in the right area, praise your puppy. They need to know they have done a good job. Puppies respond very well to positive reinforcement.

Never yell at your puppy for having a mistake (going in the wrong area). Also, never rub their nose in it. This type of negative reinforcement does not help. It does not teach them where they should go potty.

While they are learning puppies will make mistakes, expect this and be patient. If they do go in the wrong area you will need to clean it up quickly. If the odor remains then the puppy will want to go to the bathroom in that spot again and again.

There are many products on the market that are designed to help with puppy urine clean up and remove odors. If you do not have any of these you can always use vinegar and water.

Eventually you should be able to coax your puppy to walking on it's on to the area where you want them to go to the bathroom. This will be better than carrying them. You don't want them to get the idea they will always be carried to the correct spot.

Rottweiler puppies want to please—keep that in mind and the training will go faster. So even thought it has been mentioned before, we will say it again, when they do go potty in the right spot be sure to always praise them.

Here is something to be careful with. Do not take your puppy on a walk with the intention of the walk to be for them to go to the bathroom. It is best that they go for a walk after they have eliminated in the area where your training has been taking place. If you are not careful some dogs will get the idea that they are supposed to potty when on a walk and eventually that is the only time they will go. That becomes a big problem for the dog owner. Dogs and puppies should go on walks, but not with the primary purpose to go potty.

If you have the time to pay attention and work with your new rottweiler puppy when it first comes into your home it should not take much time at all to have it potty trained.

The ABC's of How to Feed a Rottweiler Puppy Properly

Knowing how to feed a Rottweiler puppy properly in their first year is very important. It is in this first year that they will be doing most of their growing and they will have special nutritional needs. If you want your new best friend to grow up happy and healthy here are the ABC's you need to know on how to feed a puppy properly.

The First Days in the New Home

In the first few days continue feeding your puppy the same food they have been eating where ever they were before. Also stick to the same feeding schedule. Over the first week to 10 days slowly begin to mix the food you will be feeding them. A good rule is to mix 25% of the new food with the familiar food at first. Then go half and half and finally 75% new food to old before going completely to the new food.

Puppies are all different and the same with breeds. You may find you have to mix the new food with the old even slower if your puppy shows signs of a loose stool or constipation.

What Type of Food will be Best for My New Puppy

There are three types of food available for dogs: dry (kibbles), semi moist and moist. The dry food is considered best. It contains less water and is not as fatty as the moist foods. It is also more economical.

There are dog food varieties that are specially designed for puppies. They contain the nutrients that are so important for proper development. Be sure to select a food that has protein, carbohydrates, fats, minerals and vitamins.

Should I Give My Puppy Milk

Milk is an absolute no-no for puppies. Puppies do not have the proper enzymes in their body to digest milk like humans do.

How about Table Scraps

Feeding a new puppy table scraps is also not a good idea. There are actually certain human foods that are dangerous for dogs. If a puppy fills up with table scraps then it is not getting the right type of nutrients it needs for healthy development. Human table scraps are high in calories and only teaches your dog bad habits.

How Often Should I feed My Puppy

For the first two weeks stick to the same schedule of feeding that was taking place where they were before. After that you can feed a new puppy three times per day up until they are 6 months. From 6 months to the first year they should be fed twice per day.

Keep in mind that a puppy will need to go to the bathroom shortly after it eats-so be sure to plan this into your schedule.

How Much Should I Feed My New Rottweiler Puppy

Generally speaking the amount of food given to a puppy should be proportional to its weight and size. For example a 6 pound puppy needs 2-3 ounces of food every day. In comparison, a 10 pound pup will need 5-6 ounces per day. Read the label of the better foods and that will also serve as a good guideline on proper quantity.

The Importance of Water

Drinking the proper amount of water is very crucial to any puppy's development and it aids in digestion.

Puppies need lots of water. Just because you are involved in potty training, don't deprive them of water. Water makes up almost 60% of the puppies weight and is the most important piece of the food puzzle. Make sure your puppy always has plenty of water available to drink.

When Should I Switch to Adult Dog Food

Because puppy food contains special nutrients designed to aid their growth, don't be too quick to jump to full grown dog food to early. Many people do this because puppy food is more expensive. A good time to make the switch is when your puppy reaches about 80-90 percent of their anticipated adult weight.

What Foods are Considered Dangerous to Dogs

There are actually quite a few human foods that are considered dangerous to dogs and especially puppies. So make sure everyone in the family knows. Here is a list of some more common human foods that should not be given to puppies: raw pork, chicken bones, grapes and raisins, onions, chocolate, caffeinated items, macadamia nuts, gum and candy that contain xylitol, alcohol, avocados and yeast dough.

To make sure your puppy has a happy and healthy life you also want to make sure they have proper health care. Going to the veterinarian can be expensive. That is why having pet insurance is so important. Pet insurance is something you may want to consider for your puppy. You can learn more by going to: http://www.DiscountPetInsurance.net.

Puppy Training - 7 Most Important Words Your Rottweiler Puppy Should Know

It is never too early to start puppy training. As soon as you bring your new rottweiler puppy home the socialization and training process should begin.

Granted, they are still young, but young is when habits and patterns start to develop that will shape them as they grow. As we discussed before, you want to train and socialize the aggression out of a rottweiler puppy before it gets very old.

There are 7 very important words every rottweiler should know and understand (at a minimum). Even as a puppy they should be introduced to these words.

Puppy training begins with knowing the correct words to use for your new dog. Here are 7 words puppies should be introduced to.

Before we go into these words you will want to make sure you read all the way to the bottom where you will find information that will help you make sure your puppy lives a very healthy and happy life.

As you begin puppy training it is important that there is consistency. Everyone that has contact with the new puppy needs to make sure they are using the same words so there is no confusion. Each of these words should also have the same behavior expectation.

1. Your puppies name is the first word that should be learned. Be positive and encouraging when using the name. You want to puppy to like their name and associate it with feelings of being loved.

2. "No" is a word that is often over used, yet important. In order for your puppy to understand the meaning of the word no, you must catch them in the act of doing something that is not good. They should associate the word no with behavior that is not appropriate.

3. "Down" is another helpful word for a new puppy. Puppies are active and should be taught that jumping up on a person is not tolerated.

4. "Sit" is a helpful word that you can start to use with your puppy early on. Teaching your puppy to sit is a very basic and helpful command. As you start to get into words like this, keep in mind a puppy will have a short attention span. So be patient.

5. "Stay" is the next word that will be helpful to teach your new puppy. Often rewarding with a small, healthy snack will help to reinforce this new word and the behavior that is expected with it.

6. "Let's Go" is a command set of words that indicates to your puppy that you want them to follow along with you. Usually a puppy will follow you no matter what you say, but using this will help them understand what they are to do when they get older and are no longer follow you just because of a puppy playful nature.

7. The words "Go Lay Down" can be helpful for puppy training when you want them to be quiet and lay in a certain area. In order for this to work they

must know where you expect them to lie down. It should be an area where they feel safe and comfortable.

Remember, in order for puppy training to be most effective everyone in the family must be using the same words for the same behavior expectation. As well, be sure to reward your puppy with lots of love and positive reinforcement.

How to Brush Your Puppy's Teeth So They Will Look Forward to it Every Time

A dog is similar to a human in that their teeth need to be brushed periodically. However, many pet owners do not brush their dog's teeth as often as they should if at all.

Not brushing a dog's teeth can lead to serious health problems. There is a right way and a wrong way to brush a puppy's teeth. Here is how to brush your puppy's teeth so they will look forward to it every time.

Why Do I Need to Brush My Puppy's Teeth?

When dogs eat they get food particles stuck in between their teeth and along their gum line, just like humans. Dogs are susceptible to many of the same improper mouth hygiene problems as humans. Their teeth need to be brushed regularly or else there will be a build of plaque which can lead to gingivitis, cavities and other teeth problems.

Dogs can get tooth aches and even lose teeth prematurely if they are not properly cared for. A dog that has teeth problems will not eat properly and that will affect its health, disposition and demeanor.

When is the Best Tine to Start Brushing My Puppy's Teeth?

At about the age of eight weeks is a perfect time to start brushing a dog's teeth. The earlier in life you can start the better so a healthy habit is established. It will be much easier to train a dog and get them used to teeth brushing as a puppy than when they get older. However it is something you do not want to rush into. You must start the process slowly so they get used to it and are not afraid.

How to Introduce Teeth Brushing to Your Puppy Properly

Brushing your puppy's teeth will be foreign to them at first. But if you introduce it the right way, you should have no problems.

First you need to get the right tooth paste. You absolutely need to use toothpaste that is made for dogs. Many of these have meat flavors that dogs love and work very well for cleaning teeth. Under no circumstance should you ever brush a dog's teeth with human tooth paste. It can damage their teeth and most dogs will resist the minty flavor of human tooth paste.

Start by putting a small amount of dog toothpaste on your finger. Let your puppy smell and lick the toothpaste. Sometimes you may have to experiment to make sure they like the flavor. Once you have found one they like, you are on your way.

For a couple of days just let them smell and lick the paste so they get to remember the flavor. Then begin putting a small dab up to their lips. Do this for a couple of days.

Now you want to put a small amount of the tooth paste in just the front of the puppy's mouth. If it nips at you make a loud, shrill noise that will tell your dog nipping is not acceptable behavior.

After doing just this for a couple of days now you are ready to put the toothpaste on a finger and touch just the front teeth with it. Let your dog lick it all off and enjoy it. After a day or so of this you are ready to spread the tooth paste on the front and back teeth, just enough so they get the flavor all throughout their mouth.

As you can see, this is a slow and gradual process that can take a couple of weeks. But if you are patient and calm and reassuring to your pet it will pay off for you in big ways. If you can brush your own dog's teeth it will save you lots in veterinarian bills down the road.

Now it will be time to introduce the tooth brush. Make sure you have purchased a tooth brush that is designed for your dog breed. At first, put a small dab of the tooth paste on the brush and let your dog smell and lick it off. Do this for a couple of days.

After your pet has become familiar with the tooth brush you are ready to use it. For the first few days only brush the front teeth. The first few times make it quick (5-10 seconds). Gradually increase the time you have the tooth brush in the mouth. Maybe one day just brush the back teeth and the next time brush just the front, mix it up.

You do not want to brush anymore than a minute at a time or else your puppy will not look forward to the event.

How Often Should I Brush My Puppy's Teeth?

The correct answer is as often as you can. You should brush your puppy's teeth daily if possible. If that is not possible it should be done no less than twice per week for the best hygiene care.

Be sure to change their tooth brush often, as soon as it looks like it is getting rough or worn down.

Here is the Right Way to Start Bathing Your New Rottweiler Puppy

There is right way and a wrong way to bath your new rottweiler puppy. If you go about it the wrong way you may establish a lifetime of horrible behavior when it comes to taking a bath. Here is the right way to give your new puppy a bath.

How Often Should I Wash My Dog?

The first thing you need to know is that dogs do not need to take a bath as often as people do. Depending on the breed, once a month or even more is usually just fine. Bathing your dog too often can actually be harmful. Bathing too frequently can damage their coat and skin and remove their natural oils.

A good rule of thumb is the smell test. If your dog starts to have a dog odor that is too strong, then it is usually time for a bath.

What Type of Shampoo Should I Use to Wash My Dog?

If you are only washing your dog once a month, which is plenty often, you can get away with a mild shampoo. Something like you might use for a baby or child would work, just so long as it is mild. The best is to use a special bathing soap designed for dogs that won't remove their natural oils or damage their coat.

How to Introduce Your Puppy to the Bathtub

Before giving an actual bath to your puppy you should start introducing them to the bathtub and the process before hand. This will help relieve any anxiety and make the event something that does not have to be feared.

Start very basic by using the word "tub". Say the word and then run with your puppy to the bathtub. Touch the bathtub and say the word. Do this several times over a day or so. Don't put them in the tub just yet.

Now place a bath mat at the bottom of the tub. You might even put some puppy toys on the mat. When you say tub this time run to the tub and then place your puppy in the tub. Reward with a treat. Some people even like to spread something like a little peanut butter on the bath mat. Do this for a day or so. Play with the puppy while it is in the empty tub, make it feel comfortable. This should be something fun they look forward to.

The next step is to run a little warm water with the puppy in the tub. Let it drain for the first few times.

The next step is to let the water fill up to about ankle high for your pup. If there is any real anxiety this is where it can happen most significantly. If the puppy squirms or looks uncomfortable offer calming words, perhaps sing to it or say "good dog." The idea is to be calm and reassure that everything is okay.

Eventually you should be able to add enough water to make the bathing process work and your dog will actually enjoy and look forward to bath time.

Puppy Washing Tips

As you wash your puppy, pour the warm water over its body slowly and continue offering reassurance. Start with the rear and work your way forward. It is not a good idea to pour water on the head, at least at first. Just use a wash cloth for the face area and ears. Make sure you have rinsed well so all the soap is removed from the coat.

When leaving the tub your dog is probably going to shake and that can soak both you and the room. To avoid this as much as possible, drain the water and dry our puppy off in the tub before placing it back on the floor. Be sure you have a nice absorbent towel on hand for drying. After drying place the towel on the floor. Many dogs like to roll in the towel to continue drying themselves off and your rottweiler will be no different.

Puppy Air Travel -The Most Current Guidelines You May Not Know

Pet air travel is growing in the US and around the world. More and more people are traveling through the skies with their pets. However, pet air travel can be tricky. There are certain things that you need to be aware of if you want your puppy to travel with you. Here are guidelines for pet air travel that you need to know.

Many airlines will allow and have provisions for pet air travel. However, each airline may have their own particular requirements or guidelines. So the best advice is always check with your airline first and ask what their requirements are for pet travel.

Some airlines, if the pet is small, will allow you to bring it with you. But the pet must be transported in an airline approved pet carrier. Be sure before you buy a pet carrier that it is approved by the airline that you will be flying with.

There are also companies that specialize in transporting your pet for you. If you want your pet to come with you to your travel destination, but you do not want to be involved in their transport, you can hire a company that will handle all the arrangements for you. They will insure your pet is transported safely and taken well care of during the flight. There are many companies like this. They can be found online by doing a simple search using the words: pet air travel.

Whatever type of carrier your pet will be transported in be sure to take the time well before the trip to get your pet comfortable with being in it. A few weeks before the trip, have your pet spend a few minutes in the pet carrier each day so it will get familiar with it. Pets like to be safe and comfortable just like humans. If they are familiar with the carrier they will be using for the trip, that will help to make things go smoother.

Make sure that the carrier has the proper identification tags on it and also any special instructions about your pet that may be required.

On the day of the flight feed your pet well before the flight. A good rule is to feed them 4 to 5 hours before they will be flying. It is advised that 2 hours before the flight give them a healthy drink of water.

Some pets may require a mild sedative for flying. It is always best to consult your veterinarian for this type of help.

When you arrive at your destination your pet will probably need to have a little exercise and go to the bathroom. There is a good chance they will also want food and water soon as well. Be sure you are prepared to provide them this help.

As well, make sure you have planned in advance how your pet will be transported once you get to your destination. Some forms of transportation do not allow pets. So you want to make sure you have this planned out in advance.

Top 4 Reasons Why You Need Pet

Insurance

Having pet insurance for your rottweiler puppy can be very helpful. It can ensure better health care over its life and can save you a lot of money.

So why don't more people have insurance like this? It is because most people do not understand how this type of insurance can be so helpful. Here are the top 4 reasons why you need pet insurance for your puppy.

Insurance for your pet is something that many people do not know much about and therefore do not have it. That is very unfortunate. For a number of reasons this type of insurance can be very helpful to the health and overall life of your pet and it can save you money.

First of all, obtaining coverage like this is not as expensive as many people think. When you consider how much a trip to the veterinarian can cost, by comparison, insurance is cheap. Insurance companies that carry pet insurance have different policies and different types of coverage, just like for humans. But a general policy that offers pretty decent coverage can cost around $15-$18 per month for a cat and between $22- $28 per month for a dog.

It is estimated that the amount of money that is spent on a dog over a life time is between 15 and 20 thousand dollars. A good portion of that is for bills due for healthcare, illness and accidents. Having pet insurance can save their owners money by covering a lot of these expenses.

The second reason to consider insurance like this is that your dog, cat or exotic animal will receive better health care and will more than likely live a longer and more fit life.

Most owners want the best for their pets, right? You are probably no different. However, because of how expensive it is to go to the veterinarian, in many cases the pet is not taken in to the veterinarian for illness or injuries when they should be.

Animals, like humans, get sick, they get diseases and they become injured. For that reason having affordable healthcare for them makes the same kind of sense it does for other members of your family. If you know the expenses will be covered under insurance you will be more likely to take your pet into the veterinarian when it needs help.

Third, many insurance policies like these also cover well visits. If you have insurance that covers well exams you will be more inclined to take your pet in for well exams. Just like for humans preventative medicine is always best. Well exams will help to catch problems when they are small before they become bigger and possible life threatening.

Fourth, as your Rottweiler ages they will need health care more and will be more prone to accidents later in life, just the same as humans. You can greatly help to extend their life and comfort in life, when they will need it most, if you have pet insurance for them later in life. There are even insurance programs that are designed specifically for older pets.

Here is where you can learn more on Pet Insurance.

10 Games You Can Play With Your Rottweiler Puppy

Playing games with your rottweiler puppy can be a great way to give them the exercise and the mental stimulation they need. Some of these may be better suited when your puppy grows a little older.

Rottweilers need lots of exercise so they are happy and healthy and not bored. Here are 10 fun games you can play with your dog they will love.

Before introducing these fun dog games, it is important to review and remind a few important considerations that you absolutely need to be aware of:

As you play games with your dog make sure you keep it fun and praise them when they do what you want correctly. If you are having fun they will too. You want them to look forward to the game and there is no better way than by making it fun and having them know they will be receiving praise.

Never play a game that might put your dog into a dangerous situation.

Keep in mind they may tire of the game sooner than you will.

When you see their attention span drifting, bring the game to an end so it does not become a chore.

Make sure your dog has plenty of water available. Dogs drink a lot of water all throughout the day. If they are running and playing they will need more than normal.

Agility Course

Using all sorts of things you can find around the house you can make an agility course that your dog will love. You will want to make sure this course offers the opportunity for your dog to walk, run crawl and jump over and under all sorts of obstacles you have set up. Be creative and use your imagination and be careful—you may have as much fun putting together this agility course as your dog will have playing in it.

Fetch

Fetch is a classic game that every dog loves to play. Find a toy they are familiar with at first throw it a short distance and say "fetch." Instinctively, they will generally go right after it. The trick is getting them to bring it back. Extend out an open hand and have them place the item in your open hand. You will have to work at this with them. Be sure to offer praise every time they do it correct.

Frisbee

Frisbee is a version of fetch where you toss a Frisbee like disc out a much further distance and as it floats to the ground they will learn to catch it in the air and retrieve it.

When learning this game practice tossing it to your dog from a short distance. Every time they catch it in their mouth give them lots of positive reinforcement.

Running Alongside a Bike

Dogs love to run, especially the Rottweiler breed. This game may take some work, but if your dog handles the leash well you can have them run alongside you while you are biking and they will get plenty of exercise. You just want to make sure they are not easily distracted and pull you in the wrong direction or run into the bike.

Hula Hoop

This game has two levels of play. At first place the hula hoop on the ground. Run with your dog to the center.

Each time you are in the center praise your dog. Eventually they will know to run to the center of the hula hoop when you place it on the ground.

Move the hoop to different spots and have your dog run to its new location.

The next step is to hold the hula hoop up and teach your dog to run and jump through it. As your dog gets the idea of jumping through the hula hoop you can begin to raise it higher and higher.

Retrieving the Newspaper

This is a fun game and actual job that your dog will enjoy. Rottweilers love to have jobs and this is a perfect one for them. Using the command "get the paper" run with them out to where the newspaper is located each morning.

Pick up the newspaper and run it in to the house. Do this for a few days. The next step is to put it in your dog's mouth and run with them back in the house. Extend out your hand like your do with Fetch. Eventually they will learn to get the paper and bring it in on their own.

Treasure Hunt

This is a game where you will hide a favorite toy or object somewhere in the house and your dog must find it. Think of a command like "where's your bone?" Every time you say that encourage your dog to find the item.

At first you will have to go to a few places and then the right spot where you have hidden the bone. Your dog will naturally follow you and eventually get the idea to look around on its own.

Hide and Go Seek

This is where you hide somewhere in the house or yard and then call out for your dog to come find you. You can simply have your dog sit and stay in one room while you go hide somewhere else. After you have hidden yell the dogs name and say "come". They will love this game.

Follow the Leader

In this game you just run all around your house, yard, in and out of rooms, up and down stairs and have your dog chase after you.

Shell Game

This is a really fun game that will impress all your friends. Have your dog sit and stay in one room. You go into another room and place a dog treat under one of several identical buckets placed upside down. Call your dog into the room and think of a command like "find the bucket". Use the same command every time. And be sure to switch the location of the treat each time.

You will be amazed, but using its very sensitive ability smell your dog will guess the correct bucket every time. You will know it because they spend more time sniffing around the correct bucket than the others.

You can even teach them to sit in front of the correct bucket, which will be very impressive. Be sure to reward them each time by letting them eat the treat they have found.

For more Dog Games Your Rottweiler will love as a puppy and when it grows up, take a look at this fun Kindle Book: Dog Games.

How to Teach Your Rottweiler Puppy Tricks

What you will learn here is how to teach your rottweiler puppy tricks.

Some may disagree that a puppy is too young to teach tricks. But that is not the case. A puppy has a shorter attention span than a full grown dog. That is the important factor you must keep in mind if you are to be successful.

A puppy is very capable and willing to learn. In fact, pleasing their owner is the desire of every puppy. Plus if you teach them dog tricks it will be good exercise which they need for healthy development. It will also help to keep them from getting bored and aid in their behavior. A dog that does tricks is generally a well behaved dog and one that doesn't get into trouble.

There are three things you must keep in mind if you are going to be successful:

Because a puppy has a short attention span as soon as you see them loose interest in the training or game, it is time to stop and move on to something else.

You must make the training fun. If you are having fun, the puppy will detect this and that will help them to have fun also. Puppies are playful by their nature and if you want the puppy to enjoy what you are doing with them—keep it fun.

You must have patience. Don't expect the puppy to learn as fast as you might expect. They will forget, make mistakes and sometimes take what seems like forever to figure it out. Just be patient and keep at it and they will eventually surprise you.

When working with your puppy be careful and aware that you are not placing them in any situation that might be dangerous or harmful. Your puppy will completely trust you.

When your puppy does something correct offer lots of praise. Tell them they are a good dog. Positive reinforcement will really help. That is what your puppy lives for!

If it is possible, you should consider picking the same time each day to work with your puppy. The pup will look forward to that time of day as something that is fun.

Be sure you understand the trick you are going to teach ahead of time. Think it through. Know what you want the puppy to do. Also know how you will show them the expected behavior. Also know the command you will use.

As you repeat the training be consistent and make sure to do the same thing every time, until they figure it out on their own.

It can be helpful when showing what you want them to do and putting their body in the correct position, to do this from ground level. It is less threatening and will be more comfortable for your dog.

Remember to be patient, make it fun and keep at it. You will be surprised at how well your best friend will respond and soon be doing all sorts of neat tricks with you.

A Puppy's 10 Commandments

The 10 Commandments of Owning a Puppy

Here are the ten things every puppy must have to live a happy, healthy life as told from the point of view of a puppy.

Number 1

Feed me twice a day a good quality food that has all the nutrients I need so I can grow up big and strong. Once in the morning, so I have energy for the day and again at night so I don't beg for table scraps.

Number 2

Keep my water bowl filled at all times. I need lots of water because I am so active. I will drink all day, but never too much—just enough so that I stay properly hydrated.

Number 3

Buy me a toy that is okay for me to chew on. I have the need to chew. It is what puppies with developing teeth do. I don't like getting in trouble for chewing on something that I am not supposed to.

Number 4

Help me get the exercise I need. I am growing and very active. Take me on walks and play with me every day.

Number 5

I need attention and love. Every day pay attention to me. Teach me tricks and things to do so you will be pleased with me and I will receive treats and praise.

Number 6

Be sure to reward me when I do what is right. The more reward I am given for doing what I am supposed to, the more obedient I will be.

Number 7

Provide me with a place to sleep that I know is mine. Make sure it is safe and warm and not too far from you.

Number 8

Teach me where I am supposed to go to the bathroom. I will have to do this several times a day. And be patient with me while I learn and forgiving if I make a mistake or two in those first few days.

Number 9

As I grow I will need friends. Allow me the ability to socialize with other dogs when the time is right.

Number 10

Be sure to take me to the Vet for all the shots I will need and a yearly check up. At times I will get sick and possibly injured. Please take care of me and take me to the Vet when I need no matter what.